Epidemic!

By Lucy Armour

Epidemic!

predict

What information do you think you will find out about epidemics?

Throughout history, deadly diseases have struck societies around the world, often without warning or explanation. Outbreaks of some deadly diseases can be controlled to stop them spreading very far. However, some diseases spread so quickly and easily that they have caused epidemics and pandemics.

An epidemic is an outbreak of a disease that affects many people in one area. An epidemic becomes a pandemic when it spreads across a large area and affects a great number of people.

No one knows for certain when the next epidemic or pandemic will happen. However, many experts believe that it is just a matter of time before another killer disease sweeps the world.

A laboratory worker holds a vaccine for the plague – a deadly disease that has caused several pandemics throughout history.

illustration showing plague victims during an outbreak in 1574

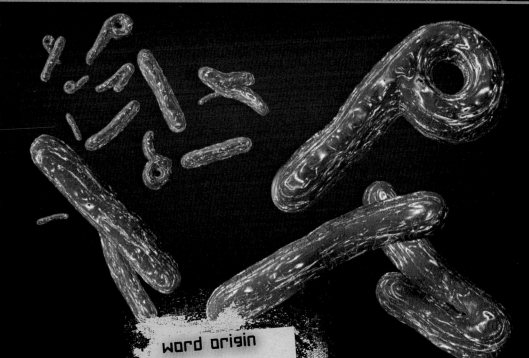

microscopic view of Ebola viruses

word origin

epidemic
pandemic
Where are they from?

The Plague

The plague is a deadly and fast-spreading disease. It has been responsible for many epidemics and pandemics throughout history, and has killed millions of people worldwide. In the fourteenth century, the disease wiped out one-third of Europe's population. It was known then as the "Black Death". The victims died a painful death. In many cases, they died alone because of the fear people had of the plague.

Today, we know what causes the disease and how it is spread. But, during past epidemics, people believed that the plague was a punishment from God.

There are three main types of plague. Bubonic plague is the most common type. A person contracts the disease when a flea bites them after biting a plague-infected rat. The plague bacteria invade the person's glands. Painful swellings, or buboes, appear near the flea bite. These buboes swell to the size of cricket balls before bursting.

Other symptoms of bubonic plague include shivering, vomiting, headache, giddiness, pain in the back and limbs, sleeplessness and delirium.

Plague becomes septicemic when the bacteria enter the person's blood and spread to other parts of their body. Septicemic plague is more serious than bubonic plague. It also causes brain damage.

Pneumonic plague is the most dangerous type of plague, in which plague bacteria infect the lungs. They spread very easily from person to person through saliva. The lungs fill with fluid and the victim suffers from high fever, coughing, chills and bloody saliva.

Today, antibiotics can fight the plague, but they have to be taken soon after the person catches the disease. Before antibiotics were discovered, septicemic and pneumonic plague patients almost always died. They usually died within five days of showing symptoms.

question

What effects do you think an outbreak of a disease like the plague might have on a society?

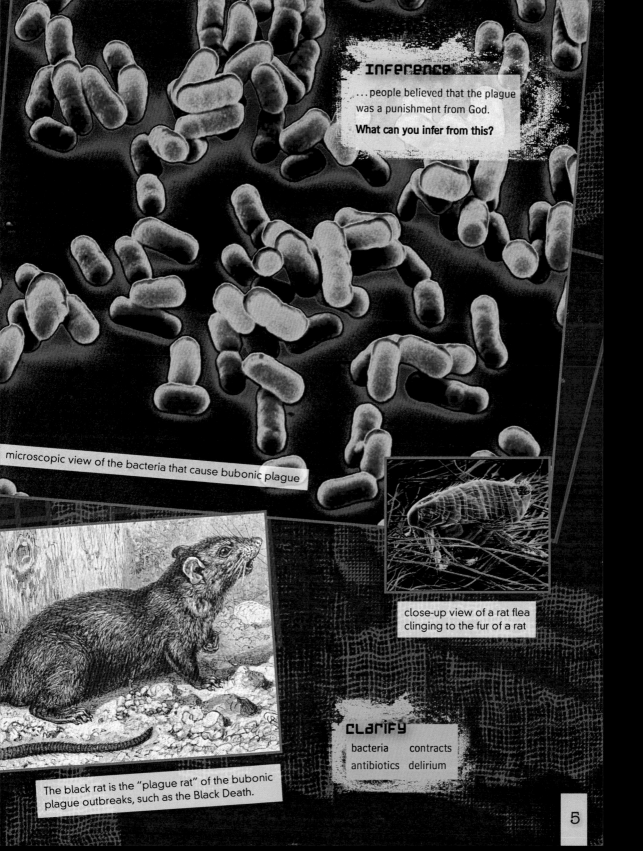

INFErEnce

...people believed that the plague was a punishment from God.

What can you infer from this?

microscopic view of the bacteria that cause bubonic plague

close-up view of a rat flea clinging to the fur of a rat

CLarIFy

bacteria   contracts
antibiotics   delirium

The black rat is the "plague rat" of the bubonic plague outbreaks, such as the Black Death.

opinion

Do you think people should have
left sick family members behind?
Why or why not?

In France in 1720 an epidemic of the plague broke out.

LA PESTE DE MARSEILLE

In September 1665, an extract from a London death register
showed 7165 deaths in one week from the Great Plague.

This illustration from the 1500s shows a
man suffering from the plague.

question

Why do you think people looked
for someone to blame for the
spread of the plague?

The plague is a centuries-old disease. It is thought to have first emerged between the third and sixth centuries BC in the area between India and China. The first plague pandemic happened in the mid-500s AD. It spread from the Black Sea across Europe. As much as half the population of Constantinople (now Istanbul, Turkey) died. At its height, the plague killed thousands of people in Constantinople every day.

In the fourteenth century, the "Black Death" pandemic hit Asia and Europe. It began in China, where it killed two-thirds of the population. At that time, many traders were travelling west to Europe, and it wasn't long before the plague spread there. Societies fell into chaos as people fled the cities. They left behind sick mothers, fathers, brothers, sisters and children.

The disease spread quickly and people looked for someone to blame. In many places, Jewish people were blamed. They were accused of poisoning water systems, and in several places Jews were burned alive or hanged. But the disease did not discriminate – Jews were dying from the disease as rapidly as non-Jews.

By 1400, between 20 and 30 million people were dead.

In 1665 in London, another serious outbreak, known as the "Great Plague", occurred. Rats and their fleas lived in the open sewers that flowed through the city, and they carried the disease with them. London's population at the time was only 460,000, but, within a year of the plague outbreak, as many as 110,000 people were dead. The Great Fire of London destroyed the city and its rats the following year and the remaining people of London were saved from the disease.

key

 overland trade routes
sea trade routes
plague outbreaks

1349
1350
1350
1350
1351
1349 1350
1348 EUROPE 1352 1346
1349 1350 1346 1346
1348
1349 1338-1339
1349 1347
1349 1348 1349 ASIA China
1320s
1349 1340s
AFRICA

This map shows the spread of the plague from Asia throughout Europe and North Africa in the 1300s.

The plague is not just a disease of the past. The last major pandemic began as recently as the mid-1800s, in China. Over the next 75 years, the disease spread to every inhabited continent, killing more than ten million people.

Around this time, scientists were discovering more and more about diseases and epidemics. Scientist Alexander Yersin of the Pasteur Institute in Paris would soon identify the plague bacterium, and the role of the rat in the spread of the disease was finally understood. Measures could then be taken to reduce rat populations to help bring the disease under control.

Today, the plague is still found worldwide and 1000 to 2000 cases are reported every year. With measures in place to prevent major outbreaks, another pandemic is unlikely to happen. However, some experts are concerned that the plague could be used in the future as a biological weapon.

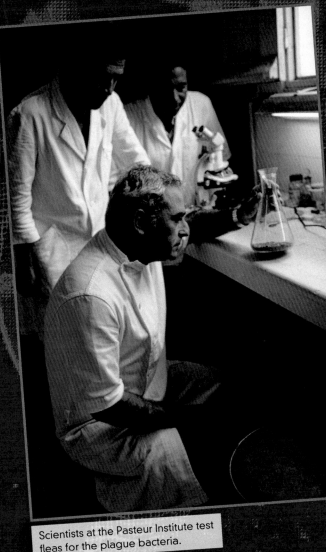

Scientists at the Pasteur Institute test fleas for the plague bacteria.

sequence Diagram: the plague

1 A FLea From a rat bites a person.

2 ?

3 ?

4 ?

VISUAL CHALLENGE
In what other ways could you present this information?

This man is spraying powder to kill plague-carrying fleas in Namibia, Africa.

question

What measures do you think could prevent major outbreaks of the plague?

Alexander Yersin

clarify

inhabited
biological weapon

Medical help is given to people during a plague epidemic in India in 1994.

Rabies

predict

What do you think this chapter might be about?

Rabies is another deadly disease that has broken out in epidemics throughout history, and it is thought to be responsible for several famous dark legends.

Rabies is a virus that is spread through saliva. People usually get it when they are bitten by an animal with the disease. Most human infections come from dog bites, but other animals, such as cats, bats, raccoons, foxes and skunks, can also be carriers.

The first symptoms of rabies are headache, fever, muscle aches, sore throat and vomiting. The disease then starts to attack the nervous system and brain. A rabies patient may experience hallucinations, confusion, aggressive or violent behaviour and sensitivity to lights, sounds or touch. They often have trouble controlling their muscles and can produce a lot of saliva, causing them to foam at the mouth. If left untreated, a rabies patient will eventually fall into a coma and die, four to twenty days after they first become sick.

clarify

hallucinations

Animals with rabies often display aggressive, frenzied behaviour, such as snarling, growling and foaming at the mouth.

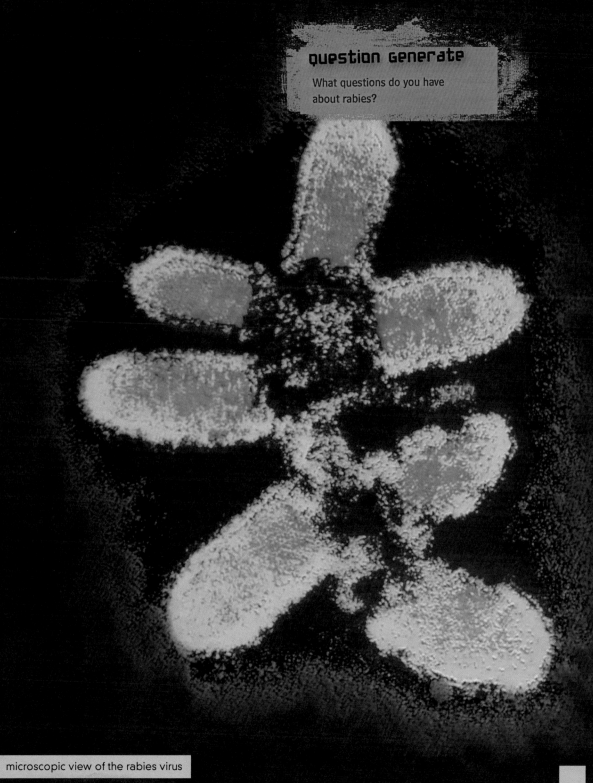

microscopic view of the rabies virus

An animal with rabies bites a person.

?

?

VISUAL CHALLENGE

In what other ways could you present this information?

Why do you think legends might have arisen from rabies cases?

illustration showing French villagers hunting a "werewolf"

CLARIFY

Sanskrit

vaccine

Three country people who were bitten by a rabid wolf die in agony in France, 1874.

The first written references to rabies are from 300 BC in India. It became know as "rabhas", a Sanskrit word meaning "to do violence". Since then, people have experienced outbreaks of rabies around the world. Some historians believe that it explains the rise of some famous legends.

In France in the thirteenth century, a rabies epidemic was spread by wolves. It is thought that this epidemic might have led to the werewolf legend.

A major outbreak in Eastern Europe in the 1720s has been linked to a vampire legend that came from the area. There are several similarities between rabies symptoms and vampire stories. Rabies patients suffer from sleeplessness, so they could be known to roam at night.

They are also sensitive to light and mirrors as well as strong smells such as garlic. Aggressive behaviour, including biting, is also common, and can transmit the disease to the bitten person. Some rabies patients have also been known to vomit blood. After death, the rabies victim's blood clots very slowly so that the dead body can look lifelike for days.

In 1884, French scientist Louis Pasteur found a vaccine for rabies. The vaccine has helped bring the disease under control in the developed world. However, rabies is still found in most countries and continues to be a real threat to human health. About 55,000 people die every year from the disease. Most of these deaths occur in Asia and Africa, in areas where people do not have access to vaccines for their animals.

Louis Pasteur

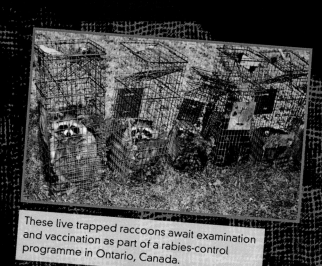

These live trapped raccoons await examination and vaccination as part of a rabies-control programme in Ontario, Canada.

Legionnaires' Disease

In July 1976, several thousand legionnaires were at a convention in Philadelphia in the United States. On the second day of the convention, dozens of legionnaires began showing flu-like symptoms, such as fever, chills and a dry cough. Several developed severe pneumonia and were taken to hospital. When the men began to die, one after the other, doctors became very concerned. Within weeks of the convention, 29 of the legionnaires were dead, and no one knew why.

All of the dead legionnaires had been staying at the same hotel. As news of the deaths spread, the remaining guests at the hotel began to flee in panic. Scientists tested the hotel's food and water supply, but found nothing.

People became worried that it could be the start of a major flu epidemic.

In January 1977, scientists found a bacterium, which they named *Legionella*, in the blood of one of the patients. By looking at other blood samples, they discovered that the bacterium had also been responsible for other mysterious outbreaks of pneumonia since 1947. Over the next several months, new outbreaks of the "killer disease" were reported around the world. The only connection that scientists could make between the outbreaks was that they occurred in large buildings, such as hospitals, hotels or office buildings.

word origin

pneumonia

Where's it from?

The Philadelphia Inquirer

Historic Philadelphia's Oldest Daily—The Bicentennial Newspaper

Tuesday, August 3, 1976

15 CENTS

Mysterious Disease Kills 16 Who Attended Meeting Here

A viral infection is suspected

Dr. Leonard C. Bachman, state health director

Dr. Philip Nash of the State Health Department gets samples from nurses Margaret Almand (left) and Debbie Schmidt

Medical detectives start the hunt

CLARIFY

legionnaire

microscopic view of the Legionella bacterium

question generate

What questions do you have about Legionnaires' disease?

the Bellevue-Stratford Hotel, where Legionnaires' disease was first discovered

1 Bacteria breed in stagnant water.

2 ?

3 ?

VISUAL CHALLENGE

In what other ways could you present this information?

Dr Joseph E. McDade (left) and Dr Charles C. Shepard (right) discovered the Legionella bacterium.

map showing some recent cases of Legionnaires'

key

- New Zealand - 2006
- Australia - 2002
- Spain - 2002
- Canada - 2005

- Belgium - 2002
- Norway - 2001, 2005
- Britain - 2002

16

Finally, scientists realised what was happening. They discovered Legionella bacteria growing in the stagnant water in the hotel's cooling tower, which provided water for its air-conditioning system. The air-conditioning had been responsible for spreading the bacteria throughout the hotel.

Legionella bacteria were soon found in other air-conditioning systems, humidifiers, heated pools and vegetable misters. Scientists now know that Legionella bacteria are commonly found in stagnant water worldwide. However, they have to be spread in large quantities to make people sick, so a man-made device such as an air-conditioner is usually needed.

Scientists have estimated that, since the 1940s, two to six thousand people have died every year from Legionnaires' disease. In 1999, an outbreak occurred at a Dutch flower show. Two hundred people fell ill and at least 32 died. In 2001, at least 449 people fell ill and at least 6 died in Spain in the world's worst outbreak. Today, new cases continue to be identified.

The discovery of Legionnaires' disease has shown scientists that there could be many more deadly bacteria lurking unknown in the Earth's soil and water. They just need the right circumstances to spread to humans as Legionnaires' disease did.

an air-conditioning cooling tower

CLARIFY

stagnant

Ebola

In 1976, in a small town in Sudan, Africa, several people began complaining of fever and joint pain. Within a few days, they began to bleed, or haemorrhage, from every opening in their bodies. Their insides were virtually disintegrating. Their kidneys started to fail, they suffered seizures and shock, and then they died. Doctors knew they were infected with some type of virus, but they had never come across it before. The disease spread to a hospital in a nearby town. There, many patients and hospital staff and their relatives fell ill. Soon, 284 people had been infected, and 151 of them would die.

A few months later, people began falling ill in a town near the Ebola River in Zaire (now called the Democratic Republic of Congo). They were treated at a nearby hospital, where 13 of the 17 hospital staff also fell ill and died. The surviving patients then took the virus back to their villages, where it spread further. Within a few months, 280 people were dead – 88 per cent of those who had caught the disease.

The two viruses were found to be very similar, and scientists named them Ebola-Sudan and Ebola-Zaire. News of the deadly diseases soon travelled around the world. There were concerns that Ebola could develop into a worldwide pandemic and that millions of people could die. However, the deaths suddenly stopped, as quickly as they had begun. Scientists realised that Ebola killed people so quickly it didn't have time to spread very far. They set about researching the viruses to try to find out where they had come from and how their spread could be prevented.

The Ebola virus is still active in parts of Africa.

Ebola areas

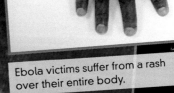

Ebola victims suffer from a rash over their entire body.

microscopic view of the Ebola virus

sequence diagram: ebola

1 A person comes into contact with an infected animal.

2 ?

3 ?

VISUAL CHALLENGE

In what other ways could you present this information?

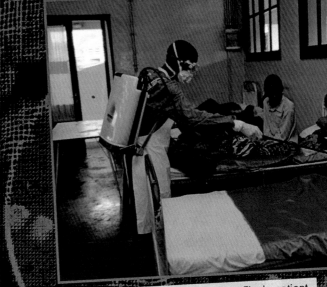

A man disinfects a bed used by an Ebola patient during the outbreak in 1995.

INFERENCE

What can you infer about the hospital staff who treated the Ebola patients?

Men wearing sterile clothing lower the body of an Ebola victim into a grave during the 1995 outbreak.

Scientists now know that the Ebola viruses were probably passed on from gorillas, chimpanzees or forest antelopes found in the rainforests in Africa. Once passed from animals to people, they spread from person to person through blood and other body fluids. Ebola spread quickly in the remote hospitals where a lack of supplies meant staff reused needles. The hospital staff caught the disease because they did not have the protective gear needed when treating patients.

In the Democratic Republic of Congo, local burial practices also helped spread the disease. Female relatives prepare the dead for burial by removing food and waste from their bodies, usually with their bare hands. By preparing Ebola victims in this way, many women caught the disease themselves.

question

What effects do you think an Ebola pandemic would have on the world?

Since 1976, many more Ebola outbreaks have occurred in several African countries. In 1995, Ebola-Zaire killed 250 people in the Democratic Republic of Congo. In 2000-2001, 224 people died of Ebola-Sudan in Uganda and in 2002-2003 128 lives were lost to Ebola-Zaire in the Democratic Republic of Congo. A total of 1850 people have caught the disease and 1200 have died. There is still no specific treatment for Ebola. Although scientists are testing possible vaccines, none is yet available. Some fear that Ebola still has the potential to become a worldwide pandemic.

A scientist wearing protective clothing studies the Ebola virus.

Influenza

On the morning of March 19, 1918, at an army base camp in Kansas, in the United States, the camp cook complained of cold symptoms. A week later, 500 people were sick and the disease had spread to other US Army camps. This was the start of the Spanish influenza pandemic. Within a year, 40 to 50 million people worldwide would be dead. The Spanish influenza outbreak is thought to have been one of the most deadly pandemics in human history.

Influenza, or "flu", is a common virus that has affected people for centuries. It spreads easily from person to person through coughing and sneezing. There are several strains of the flu, some more deadly than others. Every year, many people fall sick with mild strains of the flu, and they usually recover. But, from time to time, a more deadly strain enters the human population, and an epidemic or pandemic occurs. This was the case in 1918.

When the pandemic struck, World War I had been fought in Europe since 1914. Soon after the flu outbreak at the army camps, the US sent 200,000 troops to join the forces in Europe. Many of these troops carried the deadly strain of flu with them. Soon after their arrival, the disease spread rapidly across Europe. The flu was given the name "Spanish influenza" because people wrongly thought that the flu had originated there.

People had experienced influenza pandemics before 1918. However, during previous outbreaks, infants, the elderly and those already sick were the most affected. But, during the 1918 pandemic, young, healthy adults seemed to be struck the hardest. The virus affected the lungs and many people died very quickly. Symptoms included a blue tint to the face and the coughing up of blood. Within hours of showing the first symptoms, many patients were too weak to walk. Many died within a day as their lungs filled with fluid and they drowned.

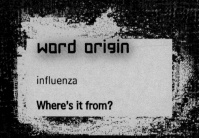

word origin

influenza

Where's it from?

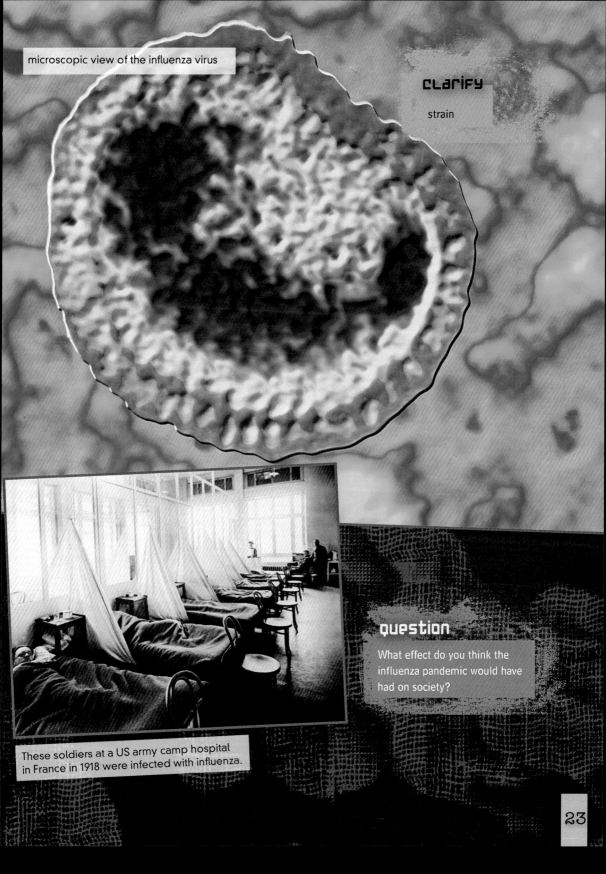

microscopic view of the influenza virus

CLARIFY

strain

question

What effect do you think the influenza pandemic would have had on society?

These soldiers at a US army camp hospital in France in 1918 were infected with influenza.

Because there was a world war happening, troops were moving from place to place and living conditions were poor. This helped the disease spread rapidly. Before long, it had spread to every nation in the world. In some places, such as Alaska and southern Africa, entire villages were wiped out. In India, 17 million people, about five per cent of the population, died. Mass graves had to be dug in large cities to bury all the dead.

The influenza pandemic was over after only a year. However, it had killed more people than the four years of world war before it, and scientists still had no understanding of why or how the pandemic had occurred.

Finally, in 1932, an American doctor named Richard Shope made a breakthrough. He studied the flu virus in pigs and discovered that swine flu, as it became known, was probably the cause of the pandemic.

In 1933, scientists discovered that there are three main strains of flu virus – A, B and C. Of these, strain A viruses are the most deadly. Pandemics occur when an A-strain virus changes or "shifts". People's immune systems do not recognise the new virus and do not know how to fight it. Because A-strain viruses can shift, it is impossible to create vaccines for them until they have already infected people.

Scientists now believe that influenza A strains come from birds. They can pass from birds to pigs and then from pigs to humans, or sometimes they pass directly from birds to humans. It is possible that the cook on the Kansas army base in 1918 had been handling a dead chicken infected with the virus.

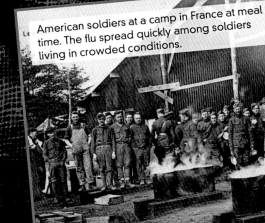
American soldiers at a camp in France at meal time. The flu spread quickly among soldiers living in crowded conditions.

In some places, such as Alaska and southern Africa, entire villages were wiped out.

What can you infer from this text?

Japanese schoolgirls wear protective masks during the influenza pandemic.

question generate

What questions do you have about influenza?

A health worker in England carries an anti-flu spray pump for use on buses during the pandemic.

Since 1918, there have been two more influenza pandemics. In 1957, an A-strain virus appeared in Asia. It spread across the world and killed two million people in one year. Scientists were able to develop a vaccine during the outbreak to help limit the deaths. But the virus then shifted and another outbreak from 1968 to 1969 took another million lives.

Since 1997, a new strain of the influenza virus has caused deaths in birds and several people in Asia and parts of Europe. People have caught the virus through contact with sick or dead birds. The virus does not yet spread easily from birds to people or from person to person. However, if the virus does change so that it can pass easily from person to person, the world could be faced with another influenza pandemic.

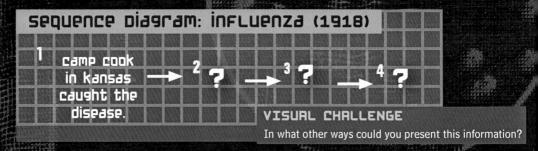

sequence diagram: influenza (1918)

1 camp cook in kansas caught the disease. → 2 ? → 3 ? → 4 ?

VISUAL CHALLENGE
In what other ways could you present this information?

A health worker carries some of the thousands of chickens slaughtered in 2006 after an outbreak of "bird flu" among chickens in India.

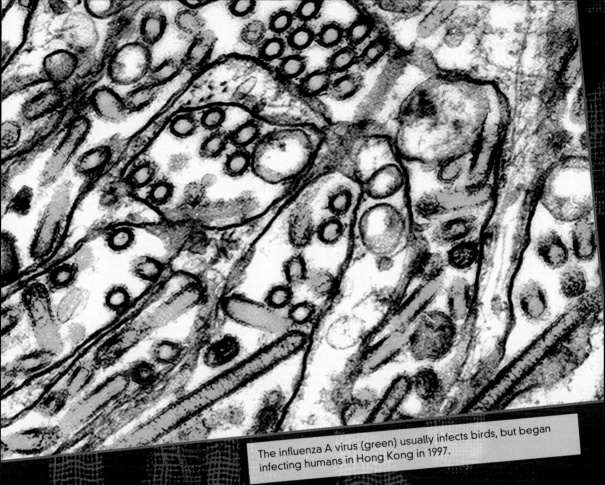

The influenza A virus (green) usually infects birds, but began infecting humans in Hong Kong in 1997.

Index

think about the text

Making connections – what connections can you make to the information presented in **Epidemic!**?

losing someone close to
you through illness

feeling fear

having an illness

text
to self

looking for answers

facing prejudice

helping people

text to text

Talk about other informational texts you
may have read that have similar features.
Compare the texts.

text to world

Talk about situations in the world that
might connect to elements in the text.

PLANNING AN
INFORMATIONAL REPORT

1 organise the information

select a topic

Epidemics

what I know:

- People have experienced many epidemics in the past.

- Some of these diseases are still a threat today.

- New diseases emerge from time to time that could cause epidemics.

what I will research:

- What effects have epidemics had on societies of the past?

- What threats do societies of today face from these diseases?

- What diseases could cause epidemics in the future?

2 Locate the information you will need

library

Internet

experts

3 process the information

Skim-read.

Sort your ideas into groups.

Make some headings.

4 PLAN THE REPORT

Write a general
introduction.

5 DECIDE ON A
LOGICAL ORDER FOR
YOUR INFORMATION

What will come first,
next ... last?

6 WRITE UP YOUR
INFORMATION

7 DESIGN SOME
VISUALS TO INCLUDE
IN YOUR REPORT

You can use graphs,
diagrams, labels, charts,
tables, cross-sections...

SEQUENCE DIAGRAM: THE PLAGUE

| 1 A flea from a rat bites a person. | 2 ? | 3 ? | 4 ? |

VISUAL CHALLENGE
In what other ways could you present this information?

Writing an Informational Report

Have you . . .

- recorded important information?

- written in a formal style that is concise and accurate?

- avoided unnecessary descriptive details, metaphors or similes?

- used scientific or technical terms?

- written a logical sequence of facts?

- avoided author bias or opinion?

Don't forget to revisit your writing. Do you need to change, add or delete anything to improve your report?